Spreading the News

Sharing the Stories of Early Childhood Education

Margie Carter
Deb Curtis

Redleaf Press
a division of
Resources for
Child Caring

Published by: Redleaf Press
                a division of Resources for Child Caring
                450 N. Syndicate, Suite 5
                St. Paul, MN 55104

Distributed by: Gryphon House
                PO Box 207
                Beltsville, MD 20704-0207

Library of Congress Cataloging-in-Publication Data

Carter, Margie
    Spreading the news / Margie Carter, Deb Curtis
        p.   cm.
    Includes bibliographical references.
    ISBN 1-884834-14-0 (alk. paper)
    1. Displays in education—United States. 2. Early childhood
education—United States—Exhibitions. 3. Early
childhood education—Italy—Reggio Emilia.
I. Curtis, Deb.   II. Title.
LB1043.6.C37   1996
371.3'35—dc20   96-6995
                        CIP

Permissions

The authors and Redleaf Press thank the following authors and presses for permission to quote from their work: (p31-32) Ginny Baum, "Documenting Children's Work," unpublished paper. (p25) Carol Brunson Phillips, editor, *Essentials, For Child Development Associates Working With Young Children*, Council for Early Childhood Recognition, 1991. (p13) Forrest Carter, *The Education of Little Tree*, University of New Mexico Press, 1976. Reprinted by arrangement with Eleanor Friede Books, Inc. ©1976 by Forrest Carter. All rights reserved. (p25) Diane Trister Dodge, Amy Laura Dombro, Derry Gosselin Koralek, *Caring for Infants and Toddlers*, vol. 1, Teaching Strategies, 1991. (p56) C.P. Edwards, Lella Gandini, "Early childhood integration of the visual arts," *Gifted International* 2:16 (1988). (p14, 44) C. P. Edwards, D. Shallcross, and J. Maloney, "Promoting creativity in a graduate course on creativity," *Journal of Creative Behavior*, 25:4 (1991). (p37) Carolyn Edwards, Lella Gandina, and George Forman, editors, *The Hundred Languages of Children, The Reggio Emilia Approach to Early Childhood Education*, Ablex Publishing Corporation, 1993. (p36, 37) Elizabeth Jones, Gretchen Reynolds, *The Play's the Thing, Teacher's Roles in Children's Play*, Teachers College Press, 1992. (p30) Ann W. Lewin, "Panels: A description of the meaning and process underlying the oversize displays of work by children," unpublished paper. (p5) Beth Menninga, *Imagine*, Minnesota Worthy Wage Campaign, 1995. (p52) Thich Nhat Hanh, "The Good News," in *Call Me by My True Names: The Collected Poems of Thich Nhat Hanh*, Parallax Press, 1993. Used with the permission of Parallax Press. (p41) Ann Pelo, "Our School's Not Fair," unpublished paper. (p62) Helen Prejean, "An Interview with Helen Prejean," *The Progressive*, 60:1 (1996). (p4) Connie Zweig, "Becoming A Warrior Writer," in *The Awakened Warrior*, by Rick Fields, The Putnam Publishing Group/Jeremy Tarchar, Inc. Copyright 1994 by Rick Fields.

Contents

Architects and Artists

When we work with sand we learn about design, engineering and problem solving.

Exploring wet-sticky textures keeps our senses alert, our curiosity alive, and our notions of cause and effect growing.

Bold strokes, gentle dabs. Painting helps us tell stories and share what we know.

Why Spread the News?

To take one's observations and images seriously is to take one's life seriously. To write them down is to offer them respect. Like dreams which respond when recognized by offering more dreams, these hunches, seed-ideas, internal pictures, and novel metaphors will respond in kind when they are given life. They will give life in return.

— Connie Zweig in
The Awakened Warrior

An Answer to Sticky Questions

Any qualified early childhood educator will tell you we are not baby-sitters! There is a professional knowledge base and a good deal of skill in our work. We juggle enough responsibility and stress to rival any CEO. Why, then, do we receive so little recognition and respect in our communities? What can we do to educate others about the value of this worthy work and to transform our worthless wages?

Other questions plague us as we go about our jobs. What can we do to counter the misguided pressure for earlier and earlier academic lessons for young children? How can we convey the importance and meaning of a play-based curriculum to parents and those who are convincing them to the contrary? Is there a way we can be guardians of childhood in our programs, despite their institutional nature, our fears of litigation, and the constraints of regulatory guidelines?

How do we quickly train new staff members who come to us with minimal qualifications in early childhood education? Is there a way to develop a sense of history and community in our child care programs, honoring diversity while documenting the learning process and engagement we have with each other?

Spreading the News represents one answer that addresses these many concerns. In an age of fast-paced electronic media and print overload, visual images supported by briefly written narratives can capture attention and raise awareness. "Documentation panels" is the term coming into favor to describe this method for communication, and *Spreading the News* is designed to show you the many uses these can be put to, the skills and tools you will need, and the results you can expect.

Imagine

Imagine a society where young college students vie to get into the early childhood program,

where a manly aspiration is to be a head teacher in a child care center,

where a family provider is the center of all eyes at a party when she says what her job is,

where a Head Start teacher's family displays her CDA diploma on their living room wall,

where a school aged teacher is sought out by a child's sixth-grade teacher for advice,

where family members proudly say that teaching in early childhood has been in their family for generations.

Imagine commercials with child care professionals selling products (like doctors and dentists seem to do so often),

Imagine how much a society like that must value its young children

when those who care for them and educate them are so revered.

(—Beth Menninga, Minnesota Worthy Wage Campaign)

Worthy Work

CREATING ENVIRONMENTS FOR CARE AND LEARNING

One of the most important skills childcare teachers demonstrate in these photos is an understanding of the value and impact of their surroundings on young children.

Skillful teachers

* design rooms that are friendly to the child's size and age,

* use color, light, and space to affect children's' moods and behavior in a positive way,

* see the environment as a tool of teaching and caregiving.

This inviting hallway to the toddler and three's room says "COME IN, YOU'RE WELCOME HERE". It was a shared project among the teachers and older children. Since two and three year old's experience anxiety when separating from their parent, this warm hallway is especially helpful at the time they're dropped off in the morning.

A teacher has converted a tiny basement space into a fine room for three year olds through attention to color, softness, and scale. By keeping things small and close together, she has built on a "play house" feeling. As a result the children are very helpful with clean up and feel a great deal of ownership in their little room. This teacher made the very best of a less-than-ideal space. (We wonder what teachers could do if they had excellent spaces to begin with!)

Worthy Work: Creating Environments for Care and Learning

In this meeting area for toddlers, the teacher has displayed a simple collage the children have made by working together. Toddlers often find it difficult to be in a group. Here, they see in a concrete way, that they have shared a space together happily. The teacher is using the environment to demonstrate their accomplishments in co-operation, inviting them into an early concept of community within their small group.

This master teacher of toddlers has worked with the children to create a large mural. Each time they find something that matches one of the color panels, they are invited to tape it to the paper. This project combines color recognition, a scavenger hunt, a chance to use new vocabulary, and a demonstration how things change over several days. When it's done, they will all help take it apart together. This environment says
"PLEASE TOUCH–
THIS IS YOUR ROOM".

Halfway down the stairs
Is a stair
Where I sit.
There isn't any
Other stair
Quite like
It.
   A.A. Milne

This room, designed by a teacher for five year olds, shows a skillful use of color to create a focal point in the circle area where daily meetings take place. Notice the large alphabet which reflects five year olds' growing, spontaneous interest in letters and writing.

This teacher has created a very clever alphabet cut from photographs of land and sky scenes. The design gives children an additional clue in recognizing letters and generates many conversations about the letters. Two children were overheard saying

"Which one is the 'W'?"
"It's the lightning letter!"

This detailed interest is possible because the teacher has placed it at the children's eye level instead of high above their heads.

Evolution of an idea

Bulletin boards have always been central to school culture, and early childhood programs have been no exception. Teachers use bulletin boards for their own creative outlets, for commercial displays related to curriculum themes, and for showing off art activities planned for children. Some programs even have regulations about the use of bulletin boards, thinking this will ensure their use as an effective communication medium.

Traditionally our favorite bulletin boards have always been focused on children's self-selected work. We've seen teachers create beautiful boards with children's individual or collaborative work displayed in ways that rival any professional art gallery's. Sometimes displays include samples of children's writing or dictated stories. There are classrooms where certain bulletin boards are devoted to postings initiated by the children themselves.

It was Elizabeth (Betty) Jones who first got us to reconsider the use of bulletin boards and to deepen our thinking about the role of representing one's experience in literacy development.

Betty began writing and talking about "the teacher as scribe" and about documenting "master players" among children in early childhood programs. *The Play's the Thing: Teachers' Roles in Children's Play* (Teacher's College Press, 1992), coauthored by Elizabeth Jones and Gretchen Reynolds, inspired us to become scribes documenting children's play as we coached teachers in their child care programs. We saw this as a strategy to help them become more attentive to and curious about children's play, a disposition and skill we see as central to effective teaching.

Then came the tremendous interest in and body of literature about the schools of Reggio Emilia, which have influenced our work. Though we have yet to go to Italy, we had the opportunity to see the traveling exhibit from these Reggio schools, which gave us firsthand experience with the power of documentation panels. We began incorporating the documentation display idea into our work with college students as well as with providers in child care programs, documenting with our pens and camera the learning process of children and adults. (For a fuller description of the role of documentation panels in the Reggio approach, see *Panels. A description of the meaning and process underlying the oversize displays of work by children.* (Unpublished paper, Ann W. Lewin, Model Early Learning Center, 800 Third St NE, Washington, DC 20002, (202) 657-4148, and Carlina Rinaldi, *Projected Curriculum and Documentation* in the *Hundred Languages of Children. The Reggio Emilia Approach to Early Childhood Education,* ed. Carolyn Edwards, Lella Gandini and George Forman. Revised edition. (Abex Publishing, in press.)

As a training strategy to heighten interest and skills in providing for children's learning through play, documentation displays are enormously effective. Within a short time of introducing and modeling the idea in programs, we found that teachers became much more interested in observing children and building curriculum plans around their discoveries. They began creating displays themselves, not just ones with cute pictures from a field trip, but displays that documented the growth of a curriculum idea and the evolution of thinking, understanding, and skill development among the children.

Soon we realized that these displays were also an effective communication tool with parents. As teachers dedicated their parent bulletin board space and newsletter energy to visual displays that told the story of the life evolving in their classrooms, their relationships with parents improved, as did family involvement and support for their programs. One teacher told us of further adapting this idea into open house for families. Parents were given a short description of a stage of play or a child development theme and sent off to study the displays for examples reflecting the descriptions. This is a wonderful example of how work with documentation panels generates its own ideas.

Our most recent work with creating display panels has been in the public education arena. Because we are concerned about the devaluation of both childhood and those who work with children, we began developing portable displays to be used in places like libraries, banks, and shopping malls. People are immediately drawn to the visual images and photographs and then become curious about the briefly written text. We add a supply of brochures related to

Curriculum News

Our Growing Project

Children learn more when they have a variety of ways to represent their thinking. After watching the children create with playdough, Teacher Melissa suggested they make drawings of their creations. As Dara sketched, she spun out a story.

" It's a machine that kills turtles. The fire comes on them. It kills turtles and breaks open their shells. These were used in the olden days and they really hurt."

NO MACHINE

Dara asked Melissa how to spell two words: "No machine" which she wrote at the top of her turtle-killing machine drawing.

Melissa told Dara that there were organizations that work to save turtles and other endangered species. She explained that people come together in a circle to discuss the problems and brainstorm solutions.

Dara then asked how to spell, "people are talking together about the machines because they are killing turtles." She drew a circle representing the people in a circle talking.

PEOPLE. ARE. TALKING BECAUSE THEY ARE KILLING TURTLES. TOGETHER ABOUT THE MACHINE.

Curriculum News: Our Growing Project

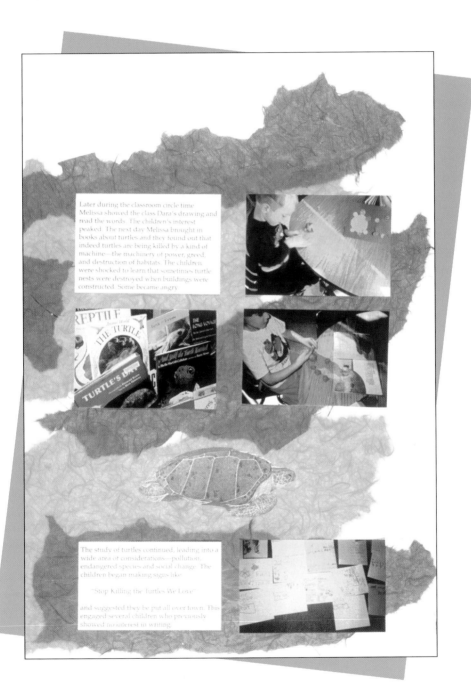

Later during the classroom circle time Melissa showed the class Dara's drawing and read the words. The children's interest peaked. The next day Melissa brought in books about turtles and they found out that indeed turtles are being killed by a kind of machine—the machinery of power, greed, and destruction of habitats. The children were shocked to learn that sometimes turtle nests were destroyed when buildings were constructed. Some became angry.

The study of turtles continued, leading into a wide area of considerations—pollution, endangered species and social change. The children began making signs like

"Stop Killing the Turtles We Love"

and suggested they be put all over town. This engaged several children who previously showed no interest in writing.

the displays so that people can contact someone for further information.

Deciding to "go public" with our displays caused us to give more attention to the aesthetic quality and professional look of our documentation. With money we received from a NAEYC MAG grant, we hired a graphic artist to conduct a couple of workshops where we practiced applying the elements of graphic design to the creation of the Worthy Work display panels. Early childhood educators certainly can't afford high-end graphic tools, but we found that our profession is filled with artistic talent that can be tapped. In fact, we have also found that providing a more suitable place to channel this talent discourages teachers from their practice of providing precut, product-oriented art projects for children, another positive outcome of this documentation display idea.

Benefiting from Spreading the News

The displays you see in *Spreading the News* represent a range of provider experience and skills. You'll find ones we've used in our teacher education work. There are examples made by family caregivers and child care teachers to document their curriculum projects and collective history, to convey the learning of individual children, and to improve communication with parents about the life of their children in the program. Also included are samples of displays created as advocacy and public awareness efforts, to document the skills and knowledge of early childhood education, and to illustrate the relationship between quality child care and violence prevention.

As we travel with these displays, people often request copies of the text to use in making their own displays. While we have been willing to provide these, we feel the process of developing a narration for the pictures is one of the most valuable aspects of creating the displays. Picture a group of child care providers coming together with photographs and stories of their daily work with children. As we discuss the thought process that goes into providing environments for children, developing curriculum, observing and setting goals for interventions and interactions, smiles and excitement erupt around the room. Yes! This is what quality child care looks like!

to show displays like these? Moving through the pages of this little book, you will find an overview of many possible uses and examples of documentation displays. We describe learning to observe and collect data and suggest ways to analyze and "broadcast" or spread the news of your documentation with visual displays. We offer suggestions about tools and graphic design tips, provide a sample release form for photographing children, and provide a sample press announcement on the availability of displays for public settings and use by organizations.

We know it when we see it. When we see it, we can describe it. In the process, we are becoming better and more articulate advocates for children and ourselves.

Spreading the News invites you to get involved in this process. Look over the samples provided here. As you study them, consider examples from your own experience. Is this part of the daily life of your classroom? Would you describe it like this or in a different way? Does it remind you of anything you have read or would like to find in literature on early childhood education? Are there other people to whom you would like

In our book *Training Teachers: A Harvest of Theory and Practice* (Redleaf Press, 1994), we open with a quotation from Forrest Carter that has influenced this publication as well: "Gramma said when you come on something good, first thing to do is share it with whoever you can find; that way, the good spreads out where no telling it will go. Which is right." Our hope is that you will continue the evolution of this documentation display idea, sparking your creativity to spread the news far and wide about the importance of childhood and those who work in early childhood education.

Making the News:
The Skill and Art of Observation

The documentation process serves to enhance and stimulate our collective memory as well as to validate on an emotional level the thoughts, feelings and experiences the group had. We found documentation to be strikingly beneficial in enhancing students' courage and pleasure in their learning.

—Carolyn Edwards, Doris Shallcross, and Julie Maloney,
authors and college instructors

The News in Early Childhood Education

At home and in group care and school settings, children reap the most benefits when we pay close attention to who they are, their interests, and developmental themes. We enhance their self-esteem by noticing and making visible their lives and accomplishments. All of this is possible through making and using documentation displays.

Teachers and parents benefit from the documentation process as well. Consider the following scenes:

Who Needs a Change Here?

Fourteen-month-old Marco has been exploring the small hinged boxes that his caregiver, Lenora, has put on the rug. He crawls to an open box, picks it up, looks at it, turns it over, and looks again. He rubs the box around his mouth and moves his tongue across the velvety fabric of its cover. Seeing another box,

Marco drops his and crawls to pick up the next one. He lingers at each box, immersing himself in the investigation with his eyes, hands, and mouth.

Lenora, busily checking the diapering and feeding charts, realizes that Marco hasn't been changed yet. Without noticing his engaged interest in the boxes, she swoops him up, puts him on the changing table, and absently takes a box from his hand. As Marco whines in protest, Lenora responds, "There's no need to cry, honey. It's time to change your pants."

No Afternoon Delight

Toward the end of the afternoon, teacher Jamie quickly reshelves the toys that are scattered throughout her toddler classroom. The children have been joyfully dumping everything out and then pushing the storage containers around the room. They like to scoot the containers close together, fill them with toys, and then squeeze in to sit with them. Jamie has tried to get the children to play with the toys as they were intended but has given up. She realizes they love to dump, push, and carry everything around the room. "It doesn't hurt anything," she says, but she worries that when the parents see such a mess, they'll think she has *no control and their children aren't learning anything. So each day, Jamie reorganizes the room before the parents arrive, leaving no trace of the children's delight for the parents to see.*

Alphabets a Must

Four-year-old Zakiya has been building in the block area most of the morning. She and some friends are creating an elaborate block structure with rooms of different shapes and sizes. Some have tall pillars around them; others are long and zigzagged. They have carefully filled the series of rooms with plastic animals.

Miss Williams calls Zakiya over to the project table to finish her alphabet book. After two or three requests, Zakiya reluctantly complies, quickly cuts and pastes a few letters into the book, and then runs back to the blocks. Sighing at Zakiya's lack of interest, Miss Williams tidies up Zakiya's book, cutting the frayed edges of the letters and pasting down the corners. She interrupts Zakiya once again: "Zakiya, come on over here and put your name on this book and put it in your cubby. You need to have it ready to show your momma when she picks you up today."

These are typical stories in early childhood programs. Not the best of news. The developmental activities and interests of the young children went unnoticed and undervalued by the teachers. Children's play is often missed as a significant focus for adult attention. Play is considered childish behavior that must be outgrown. Documentation helps teachers and parents see the important work children are doing during play.

Busy parents, leaving and retrieving their children, look for a safe, clean environment and evidence of learning in things like daily charts, worksheets, and craft projects. They have the confused notion that if they have a paper to take home each day, their child must be involved in meaningful learning activities.

Thus, caregivers and teachers, responding to these expectations and larger societal pressures, spend the majority of their time planning and directing activities. Their days are filled with continuous paperwork, preparing crafts and school readiness activities, housekeeping, and efforts to communicate with parents. With all this, teachers have limited opportunity and motivation to slow down and notice what's really going on with the children.

Changing the News

When we watch children closely, we see the excitement of scientists in the midst of new discoveries. We come to understand that while playing, children are investigating the properties of physics and mathematics, social interactions, and negotiations. As they pursue questions and hypotheses, trying out their ideas over and over again, they are mastering new understandings and skills.

Looking below the smears and clumps of paint and clay, we see budding artists, architects, engineers, and chemists, exploring how materials feel, look, move, combine, and transform. Children learn from and then use these sensory experiences to represent their ideas and feelings with designs, drawings, sculptures, and drama. Paying attention to, rather than always confining children's boisterous bodies and loud voices, we realize the skill, competence, self-esteem, and joy that come from running, jumping, climbing, and shouting.

Young children need to be noticed and their activities and interests valued and supported. As early childhood professionals, we have obligations to promote play and to counteract the pressures that stifle it. We must shift our focus from paperwork and regulations to children's needs and interests. Primary roles for caregivers and teachers should be observing and detailing what children do and then broadcasting to others why these activities should be taken seriously. More than anything, children need us to become advocates for play and guardians of childhood.

Collecting stories of children's activities and broadcasting them through documentation displays offers a method and a motivation to pay closer attention to the value of children's play. As we focus more on children and their activities, we better know and plan for each individual. We learn more about child development theory because we see it in action.

When parents see the visual stories of an early childhood program, they become delighted and confident in their child's development. Creating documentation displays provides tangible evidence of the importance and value of childhood. It alleviates parent concerns that there might not be enough learning in a play-based program.

Planning to Get the News

Collecting stories for documentation displays requires that teachers have time to watch, take notes, and reflect on activities and interactions among children. This calls for an environment and routines with enough choices, engaging materials, and time to allow children's interests and developmental themes to emerge and be documented. When children become curious and engaged in a thoughtfully planned environment, teachers have more time to watch and listen.

Observation is the Key

Teacher observation is the starting point for collecting data to create visual stories for documentation displays. Observing children is both an art and a skill. Observation skills involve an objective, detailed collection of rich, descriptive information about children's activities and interactions. The art of observing

lies in interpreting this data with an eye for the special and magical qualities of each child's development. This art can then be translated into a visual representation that captures the essence and complexity of childhood's amazing moments.

The most difficult aspect of observing is seeing objectively. Our tendency in making observations is to interpret situations and come to conclusions quickly, before gathering sufficient specific data and analyzing them. We do this because we see children through many filters. Our cultures, life experiences, values, and expectations filter our observations and information. To observe more objectively, we can strive to suspend these filters and to objectively take in what is happening at a given time for this child or group of children. This involves seeking the child's perspective in the situation.

Data Collection

We've found the following questions helpful in collecting objective, meaningful data for documentation displays:

▲ What did I specifically see?

▲ How would I name the essence of this experience for this child?

- ▲ What does this child know how to do?

- ▲ What is he or she experimenting with or trying to find out?

- ▲ What does this child find frustrating?

- ▲ How does this child feel about her- or himself?

Spend time objectively probing in depth: "What did I specifically see?" Formulating objective descriptions is a critical skill in the observation process. When you notice you have made an overly general statement, ask yourself, "What did I specifically see that makes me say that?" Try to find ways to ground interpretations with descriptive data. For example, if you said, "The child was angry," ask yourself, "What did he do that made me think he was angry?" A specific description related to anger might be, "I saw the child frown, stomp his feet, and yell." Initially try to steer away from any conclusions, so you can practice the important skill of gathering objective clues and information. Then and only then interpret the data.

Northshore Citizen

Can you see this experience from the child's perspective?

Literacy and Creative Writing

Record with as much rich, detailed language as you can. This enhances your own literacy and creative writing skills while building a resource to draw upon in developing the story for your displays. Your goal is to paint a picture with words.

Compare these examples:

Less Helpful Language

The child worked at the easel.

Helpful Language

Alicia carefully dipped the long-handled paint brush into the container of gleaming yellow paint. Starting at the top, she confidently swished her brush back and forth from one end of the page to other. She continued to cover the entire page with paint until no white space remained.

Notice the specific, detailed descriptions from the *helpful language* column. The language here gives a fuller and more engaging picture of what is happening. When gathering data, think about using the following components of language to find the best words or phases to enliven your descriptions:

Adjectives: These are words that define or qualify a noun. They add interest and detail to the description. From the example above, notice *long-handled* paintbrush; *gleaming, yellow* paint; *entire* page.

Verbs: These are action words that describe what is happening. You can almost feel the verbs above: *dipped, swished, cover.*

Adverbs: These are words that describe the quality of verbs. They give flair and movement to the description. Notice the adverbs above: *carefully* dipped, *confidently* swished.

If writing is a new venture for you or your co-workers, try working together to generate a list of adjectives, verbs, and adverbs to keep handy with your observation notepad and pen.

Finding the Story Worth Telling

When you've gathered your data and made sense of it, it's time to develop the story. This involves analyzing what you've seen and what you find important. If you have been collecting specific descriptions as described earlier, you have a good resource to start with.

As you practice the art of interpretation, it's useful to keep focusing on the child's point of view. Incidentally, putting yourself in children's shoes is always a renewing and insightful activity for teachers. It increases your sensitivity, understanding, and enjoyment of children and their development. You come away with a new respect for the complexity and importance of most of their self-initiated activities. This is the basis for formulating the story for your documentation panels.

Questions for Interpreting Data and Developing Your Story

▲ What are the children doing with the material or objects provided?

▲ What seems to be fun and pleasurable about it?

▲ How do they talk about it and represent it in their play?

▲ What experiences, people, and other materials do they connect with it?

▲ What are the children inventing/investigating/understanding through this play?

▲ How are experiences building from one day to the next?

▲ What new ideas, solutions, and answers are the children coming up with as they play?

▲ How do the children's ideas and actions differ over time from their beginning ideas and actions?

▲ What can you conclude and summarize about how and what the children are learning?

Linking Your Story to Professional Resources

There are many useful early childhood professional resources to help you analyze and describe the developmental importance of children's behavior and activities and the skills involved in the child care profession. Draw on your favorites to build your story.

High/Scope Key Experiences and Child Observation Records

One of the greatest contributions we have from the High/

Look closely:

What do you see?

HELPING CHILDREN FEEL POWERFUL AND STRONG

Children have active, growing bodies that need space for movement and self-expression. Child care providers carefully plan ways for children to feel physically powerful, enhancing their self-esteem and, sense of competence. They know that children need safe, well-planned environments and activities in order to try new things, take risks, and expand their self-confidence.

Climbing is a major developmental theme of childhood. It develops muscles, coordination and a sense of power in our bodies. Children can't get enough of it!

Look closely: What do you see?

Teachers know that children need opportunities to develop upper-body strength with things to pound, throw and catch.

Parachute play provides the chance to roll, jump, reach and stretch. It helps children explore what their bodies can do and develops coordination.

Scope Foundation is their description of key experiences— a codification of child development guideposts to help us recognize and understand a wide range of children's emerging abilities in their play. These include key experiences in language and literacy, logical reasoning, music, and movement. Teachers in High/Scope classrooms do daily planning around key experiences, record observations and translate these notes into a very user-friendly and authentic assessment portfolio for children.

Even if you are not using the High/Scope curriculum, consider contacting them for a current listing of the key experiences and their Child Observation Record (C.O.R.) system. High/Scope Educational Research Foundation, 600 N River St, Ypsilanti, MI 48198.

Emergent Curriculum

In addition to providing a wonderful window into how the staff of a child care program sorts through their understandings of emergent curriculum, Elizabeth Jones and John Nimmo's book has many examples of webbing and other forms of documentation. The table of contents includes a list of highlighted boxes for each chapter that are great to use in many different kinds of documentation panels.

Word Pictures or Developmental Profile Charts

There are many child development books and pamphlets that provide brief word pictures or developmental profiles of what children do at various ages and stages of development. Examples like the one below can be useful in helping formulate brief statements for documentation displays.

Social-Emotional Word Pictures for Five Year Olds

positive, self-confident, self-contained
sensitive to ridicule
has to be right
has sense of self-identity
may get silly, high, wild
enjoys pointless riddles and jokes
enjoys group play, competitive games
aware of rules, defines them for others
chooses own friends, is sociable
gets involved with group decisions
insists on fair play
likes adult companionship
accepts, respects authority
asks permission
remains calm in emergencies

Caring for Infants and Toddlers Book Series

This set of training manuals from Teaching Strategies, Washington, DC, covering all ages and settings for young children, consistently offers useful charts that specifically describe children's behavior and the learning behind it. The chart below is from volume 1 in the series.

▲ Things an Infant Might Do While Eating a Banana	▲ Things an Infant Might Learn While Eating a Banana
Pick it up and eat it.	I can feed myself.
Spit it out.	I don't like bananas.
Finish it and ask for more.	I love bananas.
Squish it.	I can change this. I am powerful.
Drop it on the floor and watch it fall.	When I drop something, it falls to the ground.
Try to feed some to a caregiver.	My caregiver really likes me. My caregiver likes bananas too.
Hear a caregiver call it a banana.	This thing has a name.
Try to say *banana*.	I can communicate.

Essentials of Child Development

Developed by the Council for Early Childhood Professional Recognition, this manual has clear, simple descriptions of what children are like and how adults can respond to them. It is a good resource for developing documentation panels about child development, as well as for how adults learn to be skillful caregivers. Here is one such description:

▲ What Children Are Like	▲ How Adults Can Help
Toddlers scribble with markers or crayons.	Provide thick watercolor markers and wide crayons. Offer large blank sheets of paper.
Children at this age walk up and down stairs. They soon will jump off the lowest step.	Have a set of steps made for children to practice walking up and down.
Twos love to kick balls. They stand on one foot. Older twos stand and walk on their tiptoes.	Schedule plenty of time for children to work on these skills during play. Use a rubber ball. Play soft music for children to walk on tiptoes.

Worthy Work

QUALITY INFANT CARE
PROVIDES A
COMFORTABLE, SAFE,
YET CHALLENGING
ENVIRONMENT AND
TEACHERS WHO ARE
OBSERVANT,
NURTURING, AND TRULY
ENJOY INTERACTING
WITH BABIES AS THEY
DEVELOP.

BABIES NEED MANY OPPORTUNITIES
TO OBSERVE AND PARTICIPATE IN
SOCIAL INTERACTIONS. GOOD
CAREGIVERS MAKE IT HAPPEN.

Worthy Work: Bilingual Infant Care

CUIDADO DE CALIDAD PARA INFANTES PROVE UN ABBIENTE COMODO, SEGURO, Y ALA VEZ DESAFILLA Y MAESTROS QUE ESTAN OBSERVANDO, DANDO AMOR, Y DISFRUTANDO VERDADERAMENTE CON LOS BEBES EN SES DESAROLLO.

LOS BEBES NECESITAN OPORTUNIDADES PARA OBSERVAR Y PARTICIPAR EN OCASIONES SOCIALES. CUIDADORAS BUENO LO HACEN POSIBLE.

Stages of Play

Piaget's and Erikson's characterizations of children's developmental stages provide useful references for interpreting children's play. These can be found in most books discussing their theories. We especially recommend the discussion of play in Elizabeth Jones and Gretchen Reynolds's, *The Play's the Thing* which includes a table outlining these stages. You can use the following summary to guide you in seeing what questions might motivate a child's behavior in different developmental play stages.

Exploratory Play

The child uses her or his senses to try things out, find out how things work, explore cause and effect.

▲ How does this feel, sound, taste, smell, move?

▲ What parts and properties does this have?

▲ What can I make this thing do?

Constructive Play

The child seems to have a definite plan, makes something, and gives it a name.

▲ How can I combine these different things?

▲ What can I build with these?

▲ Can I make this look like something I know?

Pretend Play

The child acts out ideas and feelings using props.

▲ What can I make this thing be?

▲ How can I use this to play a role?

▲ What can these other things and people become in my play?

Games

Children agree on a set of rules to follow while making up or playing a game.

▲ Can I turn these things into a game to play?

▲ What rules are needed for this game?

▲ How can we make this game more fun?

News with a Purpose

Whether you observe and gather documentation with a preplanned focus or chart themes that emerge from the children and the life of your program, you can create attractive, effective visual stories to capture the attention of adults and children.

As you set about creating documentation panels, consider your audience and purpose so you can focus on the message of your story.

▲ Do you want the children and families in your program to benefit from a visual display documenting their lives together, thereby nurturing a sense of history and of belonging to a community?

▲ Are you trying to map the evolution of a curriculum project and thought process that children or adults are engaged in?

▲ Is the display intended to highlight the nature and needs of childhood and the knowledge and skills of those who care for children?

Choose the focus and representations that clearly convey a story your audience can benefit from knowing. Sometimes we ask providers and teachers to gather in staff meetings or workshop settings to review observation notes, pictures, and materials they have collected. We bring brief extracts from professional resources such as those suggested earlier. Spreading things out, we first hear what staff think is significant. People build the threads of stories collaboratively and then begin writing brief paragraphs with the chosen focus in mind.

On other occasions, we assign caregivers and teachers to work with a camera, pen, and paper, watching with a focus—for instance, finding examples of play stages, emerging curriculum themes, and program strategies related to violence prevention. It may take several observations to gather enough data to create a display panel. Observations extended over time are more likely to capture the complexity of children's development.

Again we gather, look over the evidence, and begin telling and writing our story. To spread the news, we know our message must be concise and visually appealing. We work together sharing the tools and tips of visual literacy, developing aesthetic preference. As the documentation panels come together, so does the excitement, sense of appreciation, and pride. We understand that we are creators of culture and makers of history. The future is in our hands.

Children's Experiences: Seeing Themselves as Newsworthy

What panels provide to children is the opportunity to see them-selves in action, to experience the pleasure of seeing their pho-tos on public display, to study their own thought processes in these mirrors of their minds, and to revisit—and thus rethink, consolidate and extend—their own joyous process of learning.

—Ann W. Lewin

Inspiration from Reggio Emilia

The most sophisticated and impressive use of documentation panels to represent the learning and ideas of children is found in the schools of Reggio Emilia, Italy. Those visiting Reggio Emilia or seeing the traveling exhibit from their schools have been inspired to create parallels here in the United States. The time, resources and attention to both complexity and beauty lavished on the panels illustrate the profound respect and value placed on children and teachers and their activities together. This is in stark contrast to the dominant cultural values of North America.

In most early childhood pro-grams in the United States, wages are low, turnover is high, and teacher training, both preservice and inservice, is less than optimal. Teachers have limited resources to work with and rarely have paid planning time. There is seldom the equivalent of the professional support staff of a *pedagogista* or *alterista* to assist with observa-tion, analysis, and documentation of childen's activities—as there is in the Reggio schools. Childhood is valued more highly by the entertainment industry and con-sumer interests than by the pub-lic policies and economic priori-ties of our culture.

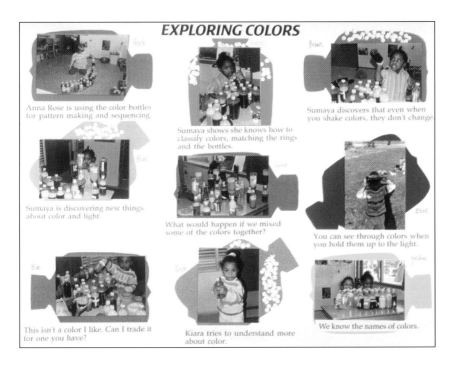

EXPLORING COLORS

Anna Rose is using the color bottles for pattern making and sequencing.

Sumaya shows she knows how to classify colors, matching the rings and the bottles.

Sumaya discovers that even when you shake colors, they don't change.

Sumaya is discovering new things about color and light.

What would happen if we mixed some of the colors together?

You can see through colors when you hold them up to the light.

This isn't a color I like. Can I trade it for one you have?

Kiara tries to understand more about color.

We know the names of colors.

In spite of this, many teachers are inspired by the Reggio model, taking the time to observe, collect data, and document their work with children. The ones we know who do this have renewed excitement and interest in their work. They are focused on children's play and development as never before. These teachers also report much greater success with parent interest and involvement in the daily life of their program.

Here's a report from one of our students, Ginny Baum, who works as a teacher in a mixed-age child care program. She used inexpensive materials such as poster board, construction paper, and markers to create her documentation panels.

I did a lot of observation of individual children to study their emerging themes. I tried to sustain their play by adding simple props. Whenever possible, I took pictures and recorded their words to serve as captions and small stories for the photographs. The children loved having their pictures taken.

I put the panels up in the learning centers that the photos were taken in. When I hung the first panels, the children were so excited. They stood and looked at them for a long time, telling and retelling what they were doing in the pictures. They wanted to know what the words said and why I put certain pictures or letters on the panels. They really liked them!

After studying the panels, they went back to replaying the activity represented in the photos. Each time they did this, they added something new and more complex to their play. The documentation seemed to help them keep building from their previous activities and understandings.

The children go back to the panels often. It's great to see their appreciation. Interestingly, they haven't tried to destroy or pull them down. Other things posted aren't treated with the same respect.

Now, when they are working on something they think is important, they say, "Go get your camera. I made something" or "Will you take a picture of me doing this?" Having the camera and other ways to document has served to spur them on to a new awareness of their own ideas and abilities.

When I took the panels down to turn in as my school assignment, the children wanted to make sure I would bring them right back. Since the panels have been gone, the children's interest in the places and materials

represented in the pictures has altered significantly. They spend less time playing in those areas and they don't seem to play with the same kind of intent.

When I get the panels back, I'll laminate them and hang them book style, like posters sold in the stores. That way the children can revisit any of them at their discretion, and we'll have a wonderful collection of what happened in our classroom throughout this year. I can't wait to see what this will all lead to!

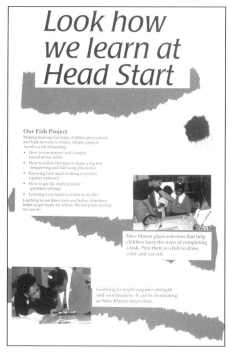

Teachers are educating parents about children's learning by using documentation panels. Miss Mason's fish project is a perfect example.

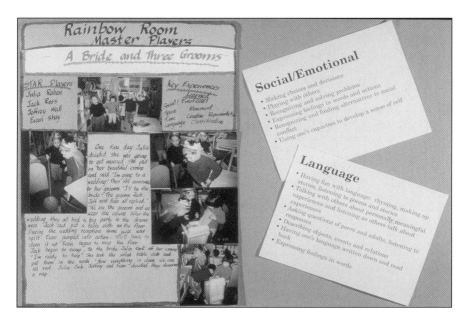

Myrna Cannon, a child care teacher of three year olds, was initially quite taken with creating "master player" bulletin board displays, an idea she learned in a training where we introduced the book, The Play's the Thing. Teachers' Roles in Children's Play. She has consistently done this ever since.

This year, Teacher Myrna has started creating documentation panels to discuss with children and parents alike. The bulk of her teaching time is spent documenting what children are doing, and representing it back to them during her circle review time. Extra photos and documentation go into individual children's portfolios and journals for developmental assessments and parent conferences.

Pumpkin Patch

In October

Around Halloween we started seeing lots of pumpkins everywhere. Some of them had faces. Did they grow that way? We needed to find out.

In our neighborhood there was a garden to explore. We asked if we could make a visit. Everybody got ready. Teacher Myrna brought her camera.

We spent all morning walking through the garden, stopping, looking and talking about what we saw. We were surprised at how many different kinds of pumpkins we saw. Some of them were so small they were hiding under the leaves.

We brought big ones and small ones back to Hilltop. This was our harvest. Do your remember what we did with them?

Trip

Pumpkin Patch Trip

"There are many different kinds of pumpkins growing in this garden. Here's a Jack-be-Little and here's a Sugar Pumpkin," Myrna explains.

"There's lots of pumpkins, big and small. We have to wear gloves to protect our hands from the prickles."

"I got my pumpkin and it's not heavy!"

Read All About It:
Sharing the News with Parents

In all cultures, people who share experiences create meta-phor—stories, songs, dances, and visual images—in order to remember their experiences, give them new meaning, and build community through their sharing.

—Elizabeth Jones and Gretchen Reynolds, in
The Play's the Thing: Teacher's Roles in Children's Play

Whither the Parent-Provider Partnership

Everywhere we go, we see early childhood programs struggling to find more effective means of communication and involvement with parents. Though everyone believes this is a critical component of quality, hardly anyone is satisfied with what is happening. There is a longing for something more, something different.

The longing we feel is about some deeper issues in our lives—lack of time, lack of extended family and community. Instead, tight schedules, traffic congestion, stresses of single and shared parenting, low wages, precarious health, and financial instability plague both workers and families in our child care programs. It seems as if we could be mutual supports for each other, but instead we typically have complaints about each other and genuine dissatisfaction with the level of communication between us.

To be sure, there are exceptions to this state of affairs, but that's what they are—exceptions. Caregivers long for the kind of respect, support, and community involvement they hear about from their Italian counterparts in the schools of Reggio Emilia. Most families in the United States don't know about Reggio, but they have their own ideas about what they want from their child's program, their worries about school readiness, and the pressures placed on them. They don't have time to read a newsletter or bulletin, help with a field trip, or attend a meeting.

Teachers and parents alike are unsettled by the expectations they have of each other.

> When I ask Robert what he did in school, he says he just played. Aren't you teaching him anything?

> When we had our parent meeting, only four people showed up. Don't these parents even care about what their children are doing?

In programs with a growing practice of creating children's portfolios and documentation displays, these kinds of comments are disappearing. Instead, there is a growing sense of excitement and a smoother flow of communication. In *The Hundred Languages of Children*, Loris Malaguzzi writes about what is needed to make an alliance between schools and families succeed:

> Teachers must leave behind an isolated mode of working that leaves no traces. Instead, they must discover ways to communicate and document the children's evolving experiences at school. They must prepare a steady flow of quality informa-

tion targeted to parents but appreciated also by children and teachers. This flow of documentation, we believe, introduces parents to a quality of knowing that tangibly changes their expectations.

> With regard to the children, the flow of documentation creates a second, and equally pleasing, scenario. They become even more curious, interested, and confident as they contemplate the meaning of what they have achieved. They learn that their parents feel at home in the school, at ease with the teachers, and informed about what has happened and is about to happen (pp. 63–64).

The idea of "introducing parents to a quality of knowing that tangibly changes their expectations" is a powerful one and not something that can happen overnight. First, the providers and teachers have to have that quality of knowing. As discussed in our earlier chapter on teacher education and training, we think documentation displays contribute a great deal to that *quality of knowing*. Second, as Malaguzzi says, teachers must prepare a steady flow of information targeted at parents.

For the quality of knowing to deepen among both teachers

Worthy Work

Providing for Meaningful Work

Early childhood teachers understand that young children love to be involved with real work— helping to carry, fix, cook, build, wash, plan and organize things. They know that children develop a strong sense of self and inter-dependence when they participate in activities that contribute to their family and classroom community. Effective teachers know that providing for this kind of involvement is a critical part of working with children.

Setting the table, serving the food, and cleaning up after a meal are all valuable tasks. Rather than just an occasional cooking project, skilled child care teachers plan and provide ways for children to help plan and regularly prepare food.

Children use real tools for cutting and cooking. They develop skills in using the tools as well as honing their small muscle control.

Worthy Work: Providing for Meaningful Work

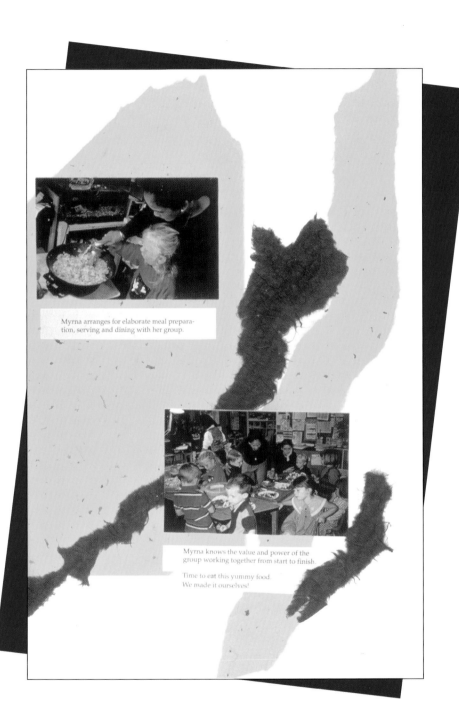

Myrna arranges for elaborate meal preparation, serving and dining with her group.

Myrna knows the value and power of the group working together from start to finish.

Time to eat this yummy food.
We made it ourselves!

and parents, we must move away from superficial reports about lunches, birthdays, and craft projects in our communication to parents. These are akin to idle chatter when it comes to the real meaning of what might be happening in our programs. Observant teachers building on children's interests, experiences, and relationships in curriculum planning have a wealth of significant classroom events to re-represent to both children and their families. The sense of history and community that grows from this shared documentation is the stuff dreams are made of. It has little to do with the generic boxes in a typical lesson plan or write-up posted for parents.

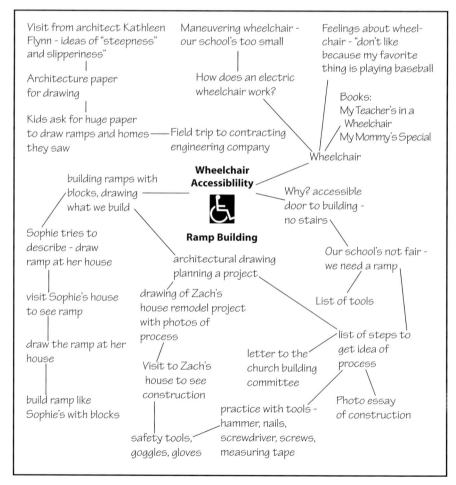

Ann's curriculum grows into a web that shows the evolution of a learning process rather than prescribed recipes. This is only a small portion of the final curriculum web.

This display (pg. 40), the full story of which is described by teacher Ann Pelo in our book *Guardian of Childhood: A Teacher's Hand-book for Planning Curriculum*. [Working title] (Redleaf Press, forthcoming):

> Picking up on the children's interest in the WHEELCHAIR ACCESSIBLE sign we noticed on our neighborhood walk, I returned to sketch a curriculum web with "wheelchair accessibility/ramp building" in the center. This was not intended to be the curriculum plan for the month, but rather a guidepost for traveling with emergent curriculum. I also wanted to begin a record of our project, our classroom history, as it developed.
>
> In the weeks that followed, I took many photos, made and kept copies of the children's letters and drawings, and transcribed tape-recorded conversations among the children. These were displayed for parents as a map of our growing curriculum. The children used the documentation as a common frame of reference and would often take out the "Ramp Book" (a display album) and tell each other the stories of the photos and letters in it.

In another program across town, (a Head Start program) Miss Mason made a visual display that enhances the quality of knowing of Tionna and her family. With a visual documentation of Tionna's disposition toward sticking with a project from start to finish, along with the ways an adult can coach her to learn the process and skills she needs, everyone can tell the story, thereby confirming individual understandings with each telling. From this grows pride, appreciation, and a desire to be involved.

Wrestling with what to do about diverse and divisive perspectives on holiday practices among the families of children at her center, Director Julie Bisson invited each family to take home an empty display board to fill up with representations of its favorite winter holiday practices. As these were returned, teachers, students, and families discovered common values as well as unique ways of celebrating.

Emergent Curriculum

'Our school's not fair'

exclaimed one of the Sunlight Too children on our walk back from the library this morning.

We were walking past the church next to the library, carrying our new books about tools and painting, when Seth noticed a wheelchair accessible parking sign at the curb. He asked why it was there. To answer his question, we looked at the church and noticed a matching sign in one of the church doors. All the doors except the one with the sign had stairs leading to them. We realized that the door with the wheelchair sign was especially for people with wheelchairs, electric carts, and/or crutches who have difficulty walking up and down stairs. The parking space close to the door saves a parking place for people who need to use the special door, we discovered.

One of the children commented that the church is fair to people in wheelchairs, but that our school is unfair, because we have so many stairs. A child in our class told about one of the people in her family who used an electric chair and who can't come into our school to pick her up on their last day. She told us that he has a ramp at his house so that we can go in and out of his house. Lee and Seth and Joel, nearly simultaneously, exclaimed that "We better build a ramp at our school!"

The rest of our walk to school, became a brainstorming time for the children, as they thought of all the things they would need to build a ramp. During lunch, while the discussion continued, I wrote down what the kids were saying.

Here's a list of the things the children think we'll need:
crane
saw
timber
tape measure
steamer
bulldozer
screw driver
hammer
crane
wheelbarrow
jackhammer
wrecking ba...
something to draw
tools
dump truck
drill
rubber gloves
cement

...

Then we thought about what place we need to take to build a ramp
here's what we thought of:

Emergent Curriculum: Our school's not fair

Dear building people in the church,

Our school's not fair. Sophie says "My step-dad who uses an electric cart because his legs don't work, he can't get up the stairs." Sam says "It's like my mom's friend Grace. She can't walk, she has a wheelchair." We want to build a ramp on the stairs that lead from outside into the Big Kids room. We want people with wheelchairs to come to our school. Can we please meet with you to talk about our plans?

From the Sunlight Too class –

From the Ordinary to the Extraordinary: Adult Learners in the News

> There I was in the pictures—just doing what I had done. I was excited to see them. Now the experience had a new richness for me. The photographs shouted out, "You did this! You were here!" What had been ordinary was now for me extraordinary. I realized how important the documenting of the experience was for me.
>
> —Ron Baer,
> adult student

An Effective Teacher Education Strategy

Whether working as college teachers, education coordinators, or program directors, we have found that representing our adult learners in documentation displays is one of our most effective training strategies. We used to go to teachers' classrooms, observe, and give them feedback. Then we realized that if we wanted them to be paying more attention to children's play, we needed to be modeling this ourselves.

Searching for ways to involve teachers in a dialogue about child development and the life of their classroom, we began taking notes on children's activities and conversations, and then discussing these with the teachers. Sometimes we would post our notes on the door, wall, or bulletin board of their classroom, bravely adding stick sketches to go with them.

When our documentation began to focus on the children and their activities, our discussions with teachers changed. Rather than feeling cautious and nervous, they became engaged, excited, and open to looking at their work in new ways. They were more interested in the professional literature we recom-

Collaborative Documentation

mended to them. Soon these caregivers and teachers began creating their own documentation, redirecting their creativity from crafts for children to imitate to displays that allowed children to see themselves at work.

It's most fun to document a collaborative effort when training teachers. We agree upon a particular focus that both caregivers and supervisors can share in the documentation process, discuss their observation notes, analyze what they reveal, and then together create a visual display for the children, other staff members, and parents. These displays alert everyone to the learning and life of the program. They teach us more and more about child development and about appropriate practices. Directors tell us that when they introduce and model the use of documentation displays, they often see a significant rise in the literacy skills of staff members who have been struggling with these issues. The overall result is one of increased communication, pride, and confidence.

Documentation doesn't always have to involve photography, nor should it be limited to special events. The point is to get

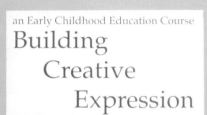

an Early Childhood Education Course

Building
Creative
Expression

Creative Expression Activities For Young Children
Ec 1.238
Course Outline

Instructor: Deb Curtis
Phone: 440-1227 (work) · 425-675 (home)
Class meets Tuesdays and Thursdays 1-2:20pm

Text: *Art and Creative Development for Young Children*, second edition, Robert Schirrmacher, Delmar Publishers, Inc.

Course Description
This course will provide you with activities and experiences to deepen your understanding of child development related to children's creativity and explore the materials and approaches that will start you on the path to be creative expression activities with young children, including sensory elements, art, construction, and dramatic play.

Class Format
Many of the assignments and activities are done during class and involve working with small groups of other students. You will be participating in a lot of hands-on experiences and working together to analyze and understand what you're doing and apply your understandings to work with children. You will also be asked to collect examples of the ideas we explore in class in your settings with children.

Course Outcomes
Participants in this course will provide specific opportunities to:

Understand what creativity and creative expression is and is not.

Explore your own creativity and make suggestions to help assess your attitudes and experiences with creative expression and how these impact your work with children.

Use observing, listening and recording to identify the developmental stages of children's creative expression, including use of materials and process or representation.

Plan and set up an environment with activities and routines to encourage creative expression in children.

Develop dispositions and skills to support creative expression activities and understand the role of the teacher in this area including:

> Prop and materials manager, Playmate, Observer, Facilitator, Coach, Broadcaster, Scribe and Curator.

Creative expression involves:

- exploring with your senses
- naming what you recognize
- representing a feeling, experience or idea you have
- developing skills to accomplish self-expression

Building Creative Expression

"I can see why kids fill up the whole page with paint. There's more white space to fill and paint left to use."

"I love the shaving cream. I love how it feels and looks as I squeeze it through my fingers."

"We have a lot to learn about ways to allow a child to develop through a creative discovery process and produce individual products and not stop the process before the product is accomplished."

Until teachers reclaim their
sense of wonder and creativity,
they can't recognize or provide
it for children.

"I've never seen anything like this before today. I'm going to go home and make this tonight."

To build creative expression in children, teachers need to cultivate in themselves dispositions of:

- delighting in their senses
- experiencing things as if for the very first time
- focusing intensely on the here & now
- finding joy, wonder, marvel and excitement in new discoveries
- exploring with a willingess to take time

This paragraph in our book really stood out for me. There is time to enjoy the process of learning. There is time to experiment, to make mistakes, and readjustments to laugh and to complete a task to satisfaction. There is also time to return to a task to re-examine and experience growth. I know I need to slow down and get out of the fast lane and keep time for my own learning process. I think these are very powerful thoughts about teaching.

"I feel sometimes we cram too much into the overall picture for one day and don't allow activities to be resumed on the following day. Some children have fallen off a cliff because they weren't allowed to explore the edges. And when they fall they aren't allowed to land in an area that supports them or lets them finish what they started exploring or the ideas they might have liked to expand upon."

"Children have so much to teach if we open to accept it. We must all learn from each other and by sharing ideas, children will be allowed to be accepted for who they are and not what they can or can't do."

Teacher education must include training in advocacy skills and strategies.

involved in observing and describing significant daily activities and presenting them in a way that captures attention.

When the caregivers in a toddler program approached us, frustrated by the amount of time it took to get children diapered, fed, and cleaned up, we realized that they didn't understand the children's developmental stage. Not seeing these activities as part of their curriculum, they wanted to get the children involved in the *real* learning of block building and art and circle time. We developed a documentation chart with a focus on "toddler self-help curriculum." Using Post-it notes, we began taking notes on the numerous ways we saw this curriculum embedded in the very activities they thought were detracting from the teaching that needed to happen.

We are increasingly using display panels in our college teaching. We make notes of discussions, draw quotations from students' journal writing, and take photographs as they engage in class activities. Like children, adult students eagerly look for themselves and their ideas in the panels.

Toddler Self-Help Curriculum

Child Initiated	Teacher Support	Environmental Factors
Casey put shoes on wrong feet.	Melanie stayed behind with Sam and Janice who were trying to zip.	Steps to the diaper changing table so kids can get up by themselves.
Jerome insisted on carrying own plate to sink.	BJ said, "I'll wait while you pull up your pants."	Children help clean with sponges.
		Mirror by sink so children can see when their nose needs wiping.

Creating documentation displays is an excellent assignment to give adult learners. It not only heightens their observation skills and excitement about children but also provides them with additional ways to address their own and students' learning styles. Adult students tell us that the actual process of analyzing their data and creating displays consolidates their thinking. Thus, making documentation panels isn't only useful in representing their learning and thinking—it actually contributes to the construction of their knowledge.

Once upon a time

...a group of adults were learning about teaching and learning.

Their instructors, Margie and John, planned a field trip to the Mercer Slough. With the magnificence of fall changes happening around them, they hypothesized that this trip would deepen understandings of nature and death in the life cycle, an interest expressed by many in the group.

To introduce the field trip the instructors "provisioned" the classroom environment for students.

• nature and seasonal objects welcomed them as they entered the school building.

• students were told the story and shown slides of the Mercer Slough.

• they were given a new and provocative tool — a jeweler's loupe — and time to practice using it.

With a map for directions and a bag of more tools (disposable cameras, sketch pads, binoculars, markers), they set off for the slough with ample time for exploration and conversation.

John and Margie explored with them, selectively suggesting the use of their tools and encouraging their adventures.

Upon returning to the classroom, there was an opportunity for students to reflect while images (slides) of the slough were shown again. This moment was followed by a brief "outpouring" of their experience, recorded by the instructors.

Students then moved to a rich environment of materials to enable them to represent their experiences — clay, collage, photographs, watercolors, cutting tools, opportunities to photocopy and more.

Metacognition of the Experience

Central to the process of learning about teaching in an emergent curriculum was an extended debriefing discussion where we explored what happened and what this meant to their own work with learners. At the heart of the discussion were new understandings about representation and why it is critical to the learning process. Representing our experience of a shared adventure provides the means for developing our thinking and constructing our knowledge.

Once upon a time

"We heard a little bird that was probably in a nest. This led to a philosophical discussion and questions or values. Do we get off the path to look for it or just listen? We chose to just listen but it was a hard decision."

"There's a dilemma in our schools. Teachers haven't had the experiences themselves that we want them to provide for their students. What can we do at the adult level to give them a visceral experience, to get these understandings in their bones and bodies?"

Habitats

wet parashol of using acrosses

Sea snell

sponge

"nose hairs are amazing"

fun former ride

moter head

"Don't ask adult students to pretend they are children. Find out what's engaging for them at the adult level."

"We have to give students enough time—almost to the point of boredom—to really uncover what is there. How do we manipulate the school system to do this? Students can't go deeper in their discoveries without adequate time."

"For someone like me who doesn't go out in nature much, I didn't need the loupe. There was so much to just take in with my eyes."

"After yesterday's field trip I have already started noticing more things outdoors. Coming to class today I saw things I never notice though I've driven that road a million times. It really works to help you see better."

today we had the chance to compose someone who might never have

Oct 1

5 briselly feet look like brushy bristles Coated in vaseline

"The feet are just amazing"

under sea creatures

Spreading the News : Strategies for Advocacy and Public Awareness

The good news
they do not print.
The good news
we do print.
We have a special edition every moment,
and we need you to read it.

They only print what is wrong.
Look at each of our special editions.
We want you to benefit from them
and help protect them.

The latest good news
is that you can do it.

—Thich Nhat Hanh, **The Good News**, in
Call Me By My True Names: The Collected Poems of Thich Nhat Hanh

Enhancing Our Organizing Work

As beneficial as all our work in early childhood is, we can't really make the progress we need in preserving childhood and play for children, improving the quality of early childhood programs, and securing respect, compensation, and adequate working conditions for providers and teachers, until some broader changes occur in the social and economic structures and the values that drive our public policy and everyday actions.

Strategies are needed on a number of fronts, and documentation panels can be useful tools in most of these areas. Whether attending a focus group, meeting, or conference, visiting or testifying before legislators, or holding news conferences and rallies, we can use visual displays to help get our messages across. The process of coming together to create documentation displays is empowering. As an organizing tool, the displays constitute a concrete project to gather around, one which builds on what we know best. We share stories, highlights of our work, frustration, and problem-solving strategies. Then we leave a three-hour workshop or meeting with beautiful displays that can be put to immediate use.

As we've suggested in our discussion of documentation panels for other purposes, it's important to choose a focus for your public education and advocacy work. If your community is concerned about violence, create a display that shows how the everyday work of quality early childhood programs and skilled teachers is also violence prevention work. If your state legislature or local school board is considering mandates for stronger academic programs for preschoolers, create displays to represent the way different kinds of play build bridges to academic learning.

The Worthy Wage Campaign has adopted the slogan, "Worthy Work, Worthless Wages," and there is much data available on high staff turnover and its relationship to quality programs in child care. People are more likely to wake up to this crisis when they can visualize what it means. Documentation displays can complement a wide range of self-advocacy and public education strategies for those in our profession.

Violence Prevention

Creating Classroom Culture with Adventure and Storytelling

Children are drawn to the violent actions of television, toys and video games because they need to feel powerful and invinceable. Skilled child care teachers reclaim power and adventure for children by offering creative experiences with drama and storytelling away from these commercial interests and the violence entertainment industry.

Role playing activities encourage children to act out their fears, gain control over their vulnerability and helplessness, and feel powerful. Role plays provide constructive expressions for feelings that might otherwise parallel violent responses.

Miss Aurora joins the children as they act out the roles of firefighters, doctors and medics. She helps them understand that when scary things happen, there are ways to get help. When children take on these "helper" roles they have a concrete way to address their fears and deepen their understandings.

"Now I'm not feeling very good. Can you help me?" I'll open my mouth and you see what's wrong."

"Let's make her comfortable and check out what's wrong."

"Check and see if she has a pulse. Can you feel it?"

"We can help her heart if it has stopped beating. This is called CPR. Let's pretend we will do it."

Preschool teachers, Ann and Sarah, borrow large, colorful masks from the children's collection of their local art museum. At first the children are cautious. They look, then touch the masks. When Ann and Sarah wear the masks the excitement grows.

As the children try on the masks their behavior grows bolder and their voices stronger. "Raaarrrmmmerrrr! We're scary monsters. But it's really us underneath!"

After all that roaring, a couple of powerful kids take a rest in the book corner.

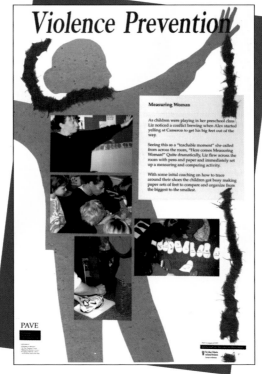

Violence Prevention

Measuring Woman

As children were playing in her preschool class Liz noticed a conflict brewing when Alex started yelling at Cameron to get his big feet out of the way.

Seeing this as a "teachable moment" she called from across the room, "Here comes Measuring Woman!" Quite dramatically, Liz flew across the room with pens and paper and immediately set up a measuring and comparing activity.

With some initial coaching on how to trace around their shoes the children got busy making paper sets of feet to compare and organize from the biggest to the smallest.

PAVE

Violence Prevention

Violence

Nurturing Empathy, Caretaking, and A Sense of Responsibility

Children need time and encouragement to explore the natural world. These experiences give them a sense of wonder and respect for life—the heart of violence prevention.

As part of her family child care program, Nancy provides abundant opportunities for the children to experience the joy and exhilaration of being outdoors. Places for hiding, bugs and plants to explore, and time for soaking up the sun. These seemingly simple activities are the essence of childhood, creating dreams and a zest for life.

A trip to a nearby farm gives children a concrete look at how things grow, bear fruit, and die—the cycle of life of which we are all a part.

PAVE

Prevention in Early Childhood Programs

Indoors in his classroom, Mr. Graft provides a large magnifying glass with intriguing items from the natural world to explore.

Child Care Providers Working to Prevent Violence

Good child care programs help children develop needed dispositions and skills to counter violence.

Elements of violence prevention may go unnoticed by those less familiar with child development. But skilled early childhood teachers plan for it daily with careful attention to the learning environment, daily routines, activities and on-going relationships that nurture a safe and wondrous childhood.

In caring for doll-babies, children learn to care for themselves along with those needing help from a more experienced hand.

WE LOVE ANIMALS
ANIMALS WE LOVE THEM
DON'T KILLING STOP KILLING

Caring for animals gives children a sense of responsibility and ways to practice being attentive and gentle with living things. Children experience the good feelings that come from caring for others. They learn to be advocates for those endangered.

Hot Off the Press: Tools, Tips, and Technology

*Images are used to construct other images—
passing through sensations, feelings, interactions, problems,
and exchanges of ideas.*

—A Reggio Emilia educator quoted by
Lella Gandini and Carolyn Edwards, authors, college instructors

Cameras, Film, and Color Photocopying

As we've discussed earlier, the first tools needed to create effective documentation displays are an observant eye, pen, and paper. Next, we advocate use of a camera and film as essential equipment for every early childhood classroom. Once parents begin to see their children regularly featured in displays, they are usually eager to donate film and even to contribute to the developing of it.

Appealing as they initially seem, Polaroid cameras prove disappointing for capturing the details of children's play. You need at least a low-end 35mm camera, ideally one with telephoto capacity. Use 400 ASA film if possible, because its speed is a better match than slower film for children's active bodies.

Shop around for low-cost film developing. When there are specials for double prints, get them; these can be used for several purposes—for instance, in documenting curriculum projects, creating individual portfolios for children, and creating displays for public education.

Color photocopying is often an economical way to enlarge and reproduce your photographs for displays. Most of the photos featured in the displays in this book use these. Again, the photocopy business is extremely competitive, and you can often get color photocopy enlargements for as low as sixty-nine cents, if you shop around.

Collecting Pictures

Taking good pictures for your display panels requires you to train your eyes. You must learn to see what the lens of your camera can capture. Your goal is not just cute shots or posed pictures of children. Instead, you want to photograph spontaneous, natural moments that represent the mood, action, and purpose of the story you want to tell.

Use a telephoto lens or get as close as possible without distracting the child or adults so that you can capture details and clear expressions. To tell a story, your photos should have continuity and show a sequence with a beginning, middle, and end. It is helpful to take several shots of each stage to ensure that you have some quality choices for your display. Photos you don't end up using can be added to the art area for the children's use.

Remember to collect or make photocopies of children's artwork or writing, along with sketches and notes you've made. Covers, quotations from relevant books, and charts you've made as part of other projects are all useful media to tell your visual story.

Paper, Print, and Signage

Depending on the purpose and technology you are working with, displays can be as simple or sophisticated as you want. For everyday displays in your program, the handiest supplies are Post-it notes, fresh markers, and colored paper. Placing these strategically around your classroom ensures that you will always have tools available to document the unfolding events of your classroom.

A simple, quick sketch (stick figures are fine) and a brief anecdotal story with children's quotations provides a good starting place for documentation. For some excellent examples of this form, thumb through the two books Elizabeth Jones has co-authored, *The Play's the Thing: Teachers' Roles in Children's Play* (Teachers College Press) and *Emergent Curriculum* (NAEYC). As these documentations show, even without camera and computer, displays of the learning and spirit of your program can be pulled together attractively and almost instantaneously.

Teachers are usually shorter on time than on talent. Once you master the art of recording observations, you may find it is not necessary to recopy or transcribe your notes. If you are documenting the growth of a project or emergent curriculum, try establishing one color or geometric shape to represent what the children initiate and another for what the teachers offer in the way of materials, questions, or guidance. With paper of these colors or shapes readily available around the room and playground, you can document the growing web of your curriculum as it occurs, avoiding the need for extra time to create a display.

Children's representations are always good to include in displays. You can add anecdotal information to samples of children's work by writing on Post-it notes. We recommend exercising great caution in writing directly on a child's work, even to record a name. Always ask if this is desired, and if so, where the child would like you to put the writing. Showing respect for children's creations in this way fosters self-respect and pride. Encourage children to make their own marks as signatures to their work, even if they don't yet write their names.

Post-it notes can also be used for brief captions with your photographs. When the pictures are developed, you may then choose to transcribe your notes in larger print or on a computer. Computer-generated type adds a professional quality to displays, but this is not always necessary or desirable.

Our workshops with a graphic artist helped us understand the principle of "less is better" in creating displays. When you choose to use computer-generated type, avoid adding too many fonts or typefaces within one display. We found that headers work fine in bold or caps but that these are distracting when used in the main text of a display with photos. For a very professional look, you can get large vinyl letters cut at a signage shop.

Design Tips

Whether for use internally or as public education tools, documentation displays are most effective when they are eye-catching and aesthetically pleasing. There is an infinite variety of individual and cultural aesthetic preferences, but keeping some basic design principles in mind will enhance your displays. Remember that in the age of

Four steps to making documentation panels

Take quality pictures: Use 35mm camera Take several shots for each Photocopy them	Collect: Children's art & writing Your sketches & notes Covers & quotes from books
Choose: Your final story line The best images Colored background papers	Assemble: Keep the "Z" pattern in mind Transcribe notes Remember "less is better"

information and electronic media, people's attention span is very short. Whether aimed at children or adults, your panels should attract potential viewers so that they will be interested enough to ask questions, read captions, and consider the text. One large sketch, photograph, or work sample from a child can be strategically placed to "hook" the viewers' attention.

In the United States, we are acculturated to a scanning motion that reads from left to right and top to bottom, whether on paper, display board, or electronic screen. Typically we are told that an effective design will keep in mind the "Z" pattern that the viewer's eye naturally

seeks and will arrange display components accordingly. Thus, a title or headline is best displayed at the top, centered or to the left, followed by a picture that represents its story. Using the "Z" pattern, the thing you want the viewer to remember most is best placed at the bottom right.

As we have become more familiar with notions of mind mapping and webbing and increasingly more influenced by full-motion computer graphics, other design alternatives suggest themselves. We can create a center to first attract the viewer's eye and then place other display components arbitrarily, in the expectation that these will be scanned randomly. In this case, there is a subtle distinction between clutter and clarity, so we follow the rule of thumb that "less is more."

If you have the time and desire to give your documentation display an artistic quality, you may first want to sketch out different ideas and layouts on small pieces of paper proportioned to the size of the final display. Cut shapes out of a variety of colored papers, then cut rectangles to represent the photos or sketches. Move all the elements around until you feel you have reached a successful design. Ask yourself, "How does my eye travel in this design? Are there things competing for my attention or not holding my attention so that I drift off? Are any important aspects getting lost?"

Torn or cut colored papers can be used to add some background movement or define targets for photos or text. Rice paper is multitextured and almost always calls forth the designer's creativity and the viewer's interest. To add variety and to tie the display elements together, choose an object or shape from the photos or story and represent it in an enlarged form with a background or accent paper.

Attention to Details

Most of the documentation displays featured here were made by family providers, teachers, and students, not professional artists. When you look closely, you see inconsistent use of typefaces, smudges, and text and pictures that aren't always cut or glued evenly. In most early childhood settings, these don't present a problem.

However, if you are seeking to refine your skills as an artist or to create a display for a public place with high professional standards, careful attention must be given to each detail of your display. For instance, pictures and text should be cut with a straight edge using an X-acto knife rather than scissors. Spray mount adhesive (used only with ventilation) should replace tape, glue sticks, or rubber cement as adhesives. Everything should be carefully measured and mounted evenly and smoothly. Removable tape (for instance, drafting tape) allows you to temporarily hold things in place while you measure and adjust. Kneaded erasers, rubber cement thinner, and fine sandpaper help eliminate imperfections, smudges, and dings.

Boards and Hinges for Displays

If you are creating portable displays, there are several types of boards to consider. Quarter-inch foamcore, 20 x 30 in., is the most standard and inexpensive. You get the best deal when you buy a case of it at a warehouse office supply store. Foamcore works well but begins to look ragged after a short time, so you may want to consider Gatorfoam, which is more expensive but considerably more durable. Gatorfoam is available in art and display stores and typically comes in 4 x 8 ft. sheets that can be cut to create six 20 x 30 in. boards.

The low-budget way to attach panels together is to use packing or duct tape on the back. This does the trick but looks a bit tacky. There are several kinds of easy-to-use hinges, but these tend to be more pricey (anywhere from three to five dollars each). They are available at stores carrying display supplies. Hinges create a significantly more professional look if you want to accordion-display four to six panels together for a particular topic. You can also experiment with scrap Gatorfoam or foamcore to create stands with slits for holding the display boards at the bottom or headers for the tops.

Arranging and Transporting Displays

If your displays are for public education, work with your local professional associations, resource and referral agencies, libraries, and community organizations to find display opportunities. Consider public hearings and events, legislative sessions, conferences and meetings, as well as traditional settings like banks, galleries, store windows, and malls.

Transporting display panels is best done in a large, vinyl portfolio case, available through art stores and office supply stores. There are also less expensive corrugated cardboard cases that provide less durable shipping and storage. For years we have used large plastic garbage bags and bungee cords when transporting panels in our car and sometimes when carrying them as luggage on airplanes. The portfolio case is essential, however, if you are shipping displays as airplane baggage or through the postal service.

Imagine: The News of a Growing Movement

I think we all put our boats out on a current, set our little sails, and when we hit something that impassions us, and our little boat begins to go there, the wind whistles through our hair, and we know we're onto something...You become alive as you're doing it, and you begin to develop gifts you just didn't know you had.

—Sister Helen Prejean, in
The Progressive, January 1996

More Than a Book About Bulletin Boards

Spreading the News offers concrete ideas about using visual displays to enhance early childhood programs. We've offered multiple examples and tips, and we hope you will be inspired to use them.

But the intent of this little book goes far beyond the idea of documentation itself. It is really a vision of childhood and a growing movement of people committed to preserving its future. It is a call to a quality of life for adults and children to become enlivened, mindful, playful, passionate, and not afraid to be awake and to live fully in our bodies. Never underestimate what this might do for our spirits and our ability to create change. Living with courage and uplifted hearts, we can turn the ordinary into the extraordinary.

There are more than 90,000 members of the National Association for the Education of Young Children and tens of thousands more working in programs and organizations on behalf of children and families. There is a growing Worthy Wage movement fueling creativity and commitment to challenge our current economic system, values, and policies with regard to child care work. Imagine! Imagine what we can collectively do to challenge and change the injustices we have been living with!

Our special thanks to those who have contributed panels, photographs, sketches, time, energy,